Sally Ride
Female Astronaut

Sage Murphy

Rosen Readers

Rosen Classroom™

New York

Published in 2014 by The Rosen Publishing Group, Inc.
29 East 21st Street, New York, NY 10010

Book Design: Katelyn Londino

Photo Credits: Cover en.wikipedia.org/wiki/File:Sally_Ride,_America%27s_first_woman_astronaut_communitcates_with_ground_controllers_from_the_flight_deck_-_NARA_-_541940.jpg/Wikipedia.org; p. 5 en.wikipedia.org/wiki/File:Ride-s.jpg/Wikipedia.org; p. 7 Orlando Sentinel/McClatchy-Tribune/Getty Images; pp. 9, 11, 13 Space Frontiers/Archive Photos/Getty Images; p. 15 en.wikipedia.org/wiki/File:Space_Shuttle_Challenger_(04-04-1983).JPEG/Wikipedia.org; p. 17 DAVE PICKOFF/Associated Press; p. 19 Sally Ride Science/NASA.gov; p. 21 MANDEL NGAN/AFP/Getty Images; p. 22 Science Source/Photo Researchers/Getty Images.

ISBN: 978-1-4777-2306-7
6-pack ISBN: 978-1-4777-2307-4

Manufactured in the United States of America

CPSIA Compliance Information: Batch #CS13RC: For further information contact Rosen Publishing, New York, New York at 1-800-237-9932.

Contents

Who Was Sally Ride?

Sally Ride made history as the first American woman to go into outer space. She was an astronaut, or a person trained to travel in space. Because of her hard work, she was also the youngest astronaut ever to go into space.

Sally was a successful person. She was a leader in space study and space **missions**. It was her goal to **encourage** people to learn about science and space travel.

How did Sally Ride become the first American female in space? She worked hard to show people that women could do anything.

NASA
CHALLENGER

Where Did She Start?

Sally Ride was born on May 26, 1951, in Los Angeles, California. Her dad was a professor. Her parents always encouraged her to learn as much as she could. As a child, she read many books, played tennis, and earned top grades in school.

When Sally was in high school, she became interested in **physics** because of her science teacher, Elizabeth Mommaerts.

Sally Ride was very smart and worked hard at her studies.

Sally almost didn't go to school after high school because she wanted to be a famous tennis player. However, she decided to study English and physics at a **college** in Los Angeles. Then, she continued studying physics until she became an **expert**.

In 1978, NASA was looking for young scientists to go on space flights. Sally was one of 8,000 people to apply for a job there.

What is NASA? It's the group of people who are in charge of space travel and study in the United States.

CAUTION
NASA
NASA
NASA
NASA
NASA

Training for Space

Even though about 8,000 people applied for NASA's space flights, only 35 were chosen for training. Training for space flights is very hard work. Sally had to study many things, such as flying, weather, math, and computers.

While training, Sally helped two space flights as part of the ground crew. That meant she helped send important messages from the ground to the flight crew in space.

To be chosen as an astronaut, Sally had to work hard at her training. She was great at flying and sometimes liked to do it for fun.

NASA

Blast Off!

At last, it was Sally's turn to go on a space flight. She was hired as a mission expert for the **space shuttle** called *Challenger*. She was chosen because she was smart and a great team player.

Challenger took off for space on June 18, 1983. On this day, Sally became the first American woman in space. At only 32 years old, she was also the youngest astronaut to go into space.

"The thing that I'll remember most about the flight is that it was fun," said Sally Ride after her first space flight.

NASA
NASA
NASA
CHALLENGER

Soon after, Sally was chosen for another space flight on the *Challenger* space shuttle. There were seven people in the crew, which made it the largest crew on a space shuttle. They went to space on October 5, 1984.

The next year, Sally started training for another flight. While she was training, a different crew took off for a mission on the *Challenger*. Soon after taking off, the *Challenger* exploded, killing the whole crew.

Sally went to space on the *Challenger* space shuttle twice. Everyone was sad when it exploded in 1986.

USA
NASA
Challenger

After the *Challenger's* terrible accident, Sally **investigated** what went wrong. She never went back into space, but NASA gave her new jobs. She wrote an important report about America's future in space. She became a leader in planning American missions in space.

Sally stopped working for NASA in 1987. She became a talented professor of physics, director of the California Space Institute, and a leading voice in the national science community.

What else did Sally Ride do? She was on *Sesame Street* to teach kids about the letter "A" for astronaut!

CHALLENGER
CRIPPEN FABIAN HAUCK RIDE THAGARD
SALLY
NASA

Teaching Kids

Sally Ride loved to teach. She thought that every boy and girl who loved science should be able to learn more about it and train for jobs in science. In 2001, she created her own company called Sally Ride Science, which encourages boys and girls to follow their dreams. Sally also wrote seven science books for children. She worked to make learning about science fun and easy!

Sally hoped that all kids could learn about science.

REACH FOR THE STARS

A Great Woman

Sally died on July 23, 2012, when she was only 61 years old. She accomplished many amazing things in her life. Sally earned many important honors for her studies and leadership in space travel. She is a part of the National Women's Hall of Fame because of her great success as an astronaut and teacher. By traveling to space, Sally showed the world that women could do anything!

Who did Sally Ride get to meet? She met with President Obama to make better learning opportunities for American students.

Life of an Astronaut

1951
Sally is born.

1978
NASA picks Sally as an astronaut in training.

1983
Sally becomes the first American woman in space.

1984
Sally goes to space for the second time.

1986
The *Challenger* space shuttle explodes.

1987
Sally leaves NASA.

1988
Sally joins the National Women's Hall of Fame.

2001
Sally starts Sally Ride Science.

2012
Sally dies.

Glossary

college (KAH-lihj) A school where people go to learn after they finish high school.

encourage (ehn-KUHR-ihj) To give help and support to someone.

expert (EHK-spuhrt) Someone who knows a great deal about something.

investigate (ihn-VEHS-tuh-gayt) To look into something closely in order to learn the facts.

mission (MIH-shun) A special job or task for a person or a group of people.

physics (FIH-zihks) The science that deals with all matter that exists in Earth and space.

space shuttle (SPAYS SHUH-tuhl) A spacecraft that carries people and supplies back and forth between Earth and space.

Index